HistoryCaps Presents:

The Legend of the Forty-Seven Ronin:

A History of One of the Greatest Samurai Stories of All Time

By Jennifer Warner

BookCaps™ Study Guides

www.bookcaps.com

© 2013. All Rights Reserved.

Cover Image © Sri - Fotolia.com

Table of Contents

About HistoryCaps

HistoryCaps is an imprint of BookCaps™ Study Guides. With each book, a brief period of history is recapped. We publish a wide array of topics (from baseball and music to science and philosophy), so check our growing catalogue regularly (**www.bookcaps.com**) to see our newest books.

Revenge. Murder. Honor. These are the ingredients of one of the greatest samurai legends of all time: The Forty-Seven Ronin—the legend of samurai who take revenge on a court official who leaves them leaderless.

With a gripping narrative, HistoryCaps takes you back in time for a look at perhaps the greatest samurai tales in the history of Japan.

Introduction

Honor. Discipline. Courage. Now that the time had come Asano Naganori struggled in vain to focus on samurai virtues. He tried to summon up the lessons drummed into his head in his youth, but they had long since vanished from his memory.

Controlling his breath he exhaled silently as he stepped into the servants' courtyard of Edo Castle. It flashed through his mind what folly it had been to leave behind in distant Akō his most faithful and highest ranking retainer. He would have to rely on his second-in-command, Yoshida Chuzaemon Kanesuke to ensure that his honor was retained in the brief ritual. The 62-year-old Yoshida, who had distinguished himself only in minor battles, followed his master at a distance of two paces. Behind him marched the best swordsman in his service. A small contingent of Asano's fully armored warriors followed. They halted in the middle of the courtyard as Asano, Yoshida and the swordsman disappeared through the open and unattended Impure Gate, the passage from Edo Castle reserved for corpses and criminals.

Asano walked into the garden beyond the walls where a reed mat had been laid out on the gravel. In sentencing him, the Shogun's inspectors made a point of denying him the use of the grand chamber for the ritual. It was his right, he believed, as a daimyo or territorial lord to perform the ritual within the castle. The inspectors had resisted reversing their decision, rejecting every entreaty put forth by the daimyo's retainers.

With his eyes firmly fixed on a patch of curling bark on a cherry tree a few paces away, Asano knelt on the mat placing his knees precisely a fist-width apart. Yoshida stepped back, and the swordsman took his place behind his master. Without shifting his gaze, the daimyo of Akō solemnly untied the sash of his white kimono and pulled it back to bare his torso. Bending gracefully forward he methodically tucked the cuffs of his garment under his knees and gracefully grasped the hilt of the unsheathed knife set out on a small wooden stand. With his left hand, he reached across his body and plucked a square of white cloth from the glazed porcelain basin next to his right knee. He wrapped the cloth three times around the upper part of the blade and gripped it tightly in his right hand. He hesitated for a second then without looking down plunged the knife into his abdomen and pulled it abruptly to the right. The swordsman standing behind tensed his muscles. When he heard the sound of Asano's bowels spilling out from the gash, he swung his weapon neatly severing his master's head, leaving a bit of skin uncut at the throat. Asano's hinged head fell forward onto his chest. His decapitated body remained vertical for several seconds then toppled forward onto the matt already darkened by rivulets of blood converging on an expanding brilliant red puddle.

The samurai captain had successfully honored his master maintaining disciplined composure as he focussed on the seppuku ritual. Without moving his eyes from the body of Asano, Yoshida raised his right hand signaling the waiting warriors clustered inside the Impure Gate. The hand-picked group marched forward and formed a circle around their master's body. The captain signalled again with his hand and four of the samurai stepped forward and knelt on the ground to Asano's body. One of them unclasped the lifeless hands from the seppuku dagger, lifted up and placed it in Yoshida's outstretched hand. The warriors tenderly rolled Asano's corpse over. One of them pushed his organs back into the gash in belly. Another retrieved the head, which had come loose and rolled off the mat, and placed it on Asano's chest. The four samurai slowly lifted their master's body over their heads paused a moment before depositing the corpse on a white silk shroud laid out on the ground nearby. They wrapped him tightly, raised the body to their shoulders and on a silent signal from Yoshida took the first step in the solemn procession through the streets of Edo to deliver their master's corpse to Sengakuji temple.

From the moment, they were told of the sentencing of Asano to seppuku and during the ritual of his death, sombre funeral procession and the ceremonial washing of his body at the temple, all of the daimyo's samurai warriors maintained the kind of disciplined fortitude set out in bushidō code of behavior.

8

Established in the 12th century as an ethical way of life for the samurai, bushidō combined elements of Shinto, Confucian and Zen Buddhist moral precepts. The hereditary warrior class of samurai served their master with absolute loyalty thus ensuring his protection in a period of constant warfare between contending lords of Japan. Bushidō demanded rectitude or righteousness, courage, benevolence or compassion, respect, honesty, honor and loyalty.

In 1701 when Asano performed seppuku, Japan, under the Shogun Tsunayoshi, who had ruled since 1680, was changing dramatically. The Shogun's samurai warriors and those loyal to his vassal lords or daimyo did not support themselves as they had once done by income from farms on lands given them by their master's. Rather they lived in the castle towns of the daimyo and were paid salaries for their service. In this way, they were directly under the control of their master who could offer monetary rewards for whatever kind of service he wished even if it went against the bushidō code.

The all-powerful Shogun could not always control the warlike behavior of his vassals. As with all political leaders, even autocrats, he was unable to wipe out corruption on their estates, and he was continually on guard anticipating lapses in loyalty among officials in his own government or bakufu. One of the ways the Shogun employed to minimize the penchant for war was to require each of his vassal lords to take up residence for part of the year in his capital city of Edo. The daimyo thus moved back and forth between Edo and their provincial domains. Keeping two grand houses was costly and time consuming and the movement between the two residences often involved long journeys with retinues of household retainers and samurai. This back and forth travel with supplies to feed many people reduced the capacity of the daimyo to engage in warfare with each other.

Asano Naganori, whose castle was at Akō some 600 miles from Edo, did not have a reputation in the capital as an honorable man. Long before he ran afoul of the bakufu, or feudal, military dictatorship of the Shogun, it was reported to the administration that while he was intelligent and quick to punish wrong-doers on his estates, he was a pleasure seeker and an egotistical womanizer. Asano was also criticized for misusing his feudal authority demanding from his vassal farmers more than his share of their best produce and rewarding his samurai for their procurement of women from his estates for his gratification. His warriors bound by absolute loyalty provided for his every whim and turned a blind eye to corruption in his domain.

In Asano's time, the need for large numbers of fighting men had diminished. For the most part under the central power of Tokugawa shogunate from 1603 to 1868, also known as the Edo period, there was peace in Japan. The samurai class or caste thus took on administrative roles in the Shogun's court and in the households of the regional lords. The Shogun's samurai adviser who prepared the report on Asano placed the blame for his bad behavior on the shoulders of his principal retainer Oishi Kuranosuke Yoshikatsu. He was taken to task for failing to train his master in the correct way of living. Asano lacked interest and knowledge of the highly esteemed artistic and literary worlds and had acquired only marginal military skills. Some have suggested that Oishi was a bit obsequious and enjoyed his role of being the power behind his dissolute master. Nicknamed Lord Daytime Paper Lantern or useless person, Oishi was a poor manager of money and had a passion for drinking. The state of affairs in Akō was proof of an observation made by the poet and warrior Imagawa Ryōshun who wrote in the 15th century; "Therefore it is said that the master who governs his domain well loves wise retainers, while the man who exploits the people loves flatterers."

There was little excuse for the flaws in the characters of Asano and Oishi because they both had one of the most astute teachers of the time. The philosopher Yamaga Sokō had settled in Akō after being relieved of his position in the bureaucracy of the Shogun. His ideas conflicted with the accepted doctrines of the government in Edo. He outlined his unorthodox concepts in essays on the warrior creed or bukyō and the way of the gentleman or shidō. He stated that shidō demanded absolute purity of a warrior and commitment to serve as an example to other classes and that the samurai must punish those who stray from the path of purity. Yamaga said that the intellectual training of a samurai must include the arts, writing and history. He believed that a samurai must be much more than a warrior and become an intellectual and political leader. It is doubtful that Asano and Oishi truly understood their teacher and his lessons on the ethical teachings of Confucius and their role in the bushidō way of life.

Chapter 1: The Tragedy

The story of Asano Naganori's route to seppuku and what happened after his death has become the national legend of Japan. Like most ancient stories, the historical truth is elusive. The facts have been twisted, turned, modified, revised and reconstructed. What transpired has, over the years, been manipulated so that the tale confirm whatever beliefs and fashion are current at the time of the telling. The story as it is presented here is of necessity a compilation of historically accurate information with generous doses of unverifiable speculation. In this, it follows in the tradition of Japanese storytelling.

When the events of the narrative took place, Shogun Tsunayoshi was the military and sole autocratic authority in Japan. The Emperor, who lived in a castle in Kyoto, held the highest office, but his authority was manifest only in ceremony much like a modern constitutional monarchy. In spite of the fact that the Emperor's power over daily life in Japan was strictly limited he was treated with extreme deference. The ancient customs of court life were followed to the letter so that when a messenger was sent from the Emperor to the Shogun announcing that he was dispatching two ambassadors to the Shogun's court in Edo, Tsunayoshi's administrators set to work preparing for the intricate formalities of the visit.

Two daimyo then serving their period of residency in Edo were selected to greet and entertain the Emperor's ambassadors. Asano Naganori and Kamei Sama were ordered to attend daily lessons in the castle to learn the details of court etiquette so that they could provide proper hospitality to the visiting dignitaries. They were to be taught the precise protocols for greeting and meeting representatives of the Imperial court by one of the Shogun's knowledgeable retainers named Kira Yoshinaka. Kira had served in the bakufu for about 40 years as part of a group of bureaucrats called koke or high families responsible for court ceremony. The longevity of his service indicates that he was good at his job. His master, the Shogun, was extremely demanding and was noted for his habit of demoting and promoting his retainers on a whim. Like the Queen of Hearts in *Alice in Wonderland* he was capricious and what might seem to us today as minor errors led to the command "off with his head."

Kira himself was as severe as his overlord. He was pompous and possessed a sharp tongue in his dealings with those he considered to be of inferior status. His attitude toward the two daimyo students was far from polite. As a sophisticate in courtly life, he considered his charges to be uncultured country bumpkins. It was his duty to smooth their rough edges and transform the daimyo into refined courtiers.

When their first lesson began Asano and Kamei, ignorant of the ways of court or more likely habitually cheap, failed to deliver to Kira appropriate gifts for his services. Kira, as with all court retainers received a salary that was inadequate to support him in the style required of a member of the bakufu. It was expected that his income would be supplemented by appropriate gifts or bribes by those to whom he rendered service. Mere token payments were justly regarded as an insult. Like a waiter serving a repeat customer with a reputation as a stingy tipper, Kira, was mean and condescending to his students.

The three did not get along, and as with any dispute between a teacher and student their relationship went from bad to worse. Kira seems to have been fond of making fun of his students' ignorance taunting them with sarcasm over such triffles as the way they tied their sashes, bowed their heads or recited the formal words necessary in greeting an honored guest. One day after class while walking to their Edo mansions Kamei Sama announced to Asano that he was so infuriated with being the brunt of Kira's sarcasm that he was going to kill the vile instructor at the next class.

When he got home Kamei announced to his councillors, a retinue of his most trusted samurai, his decision to do away with Kira. He said that he was well aware that killing the annoying instructor would have severe repercussions on his household. His properties would be confiscated by the Shogun, his samurai and household retainers would be dismissed, and he would have to forfeit his life. In spite of the consequences of going through with the planned assassination, he became more and more enraged as he reiterated his determination to end his humiliation. The wisest of his unquestionably loyal and respectful retainers stated that the daimyo's word was law and that he and his warriors' were unwavering in their support. This was a demonstration of the complete selflessness of the samurai as they all knew that when their master paid with his life for the murder of the teacher they would be cast loose into the world and as rōnin or masterless samurai would be forced to hire themselves out to a new daimyo or make a living as merchants or even worse a craftsmen or farmers.

The wise councillor went to his home and decided to rectify the situation by secretly paying, on behalf of his master, a bribe to Kira. He collected his personal savings and sent a servant to the Shogun's castle with a bag of silver. The servant presented the bribe to Kira with a well prepared formal speech apologizing for the late gift and praising the teacher with an abundance of well-chosen flattering words.

The next day, April 21, 1701, still seething with anger and harboring homicidal intentions, Kamei went to the castle before the day's lessons were to begin. When Kira strode into the chamber they had been using as a classroom, Kamei's demonstration of wrath was pre-empted by pacifying words uttered by Kamei who begged forgiveness for his rudeness. He promised to proceed with the instruction of Kamei in the intricacies of diplomacy and court comportment with benevolence, generosity and compassion required by the code of bushidō. Kamei who did not know why this change of heart had come about accepted his teacher's apologies and abandoned his murderous intentions.

When Asano Naganori arrived at the castle, and the daily etiquette lessons began he was the brunt of even greater taunts from Kira. Lifting his leg he pointed to the ribbon on his sock that had come undone and demanded that Asano retie it. Usually inattentive to the lesson at hand Asano did not immediately respond to the order.

"Pay attention lazy country boy," Kira shouted, "tie the ribbon as I have commanded."

Asano's face flushed with anger. He bit his lip and lowered his corpulent body. Struggling to kneel before Kira he retied the ribbon with trembling fingers.

"Not that way you lout. Where on earth did you learn to tie up a stocking? What kind of house do you have here in Edo. I can imagine that you have dirt on your hands and live in filth and squalor on your lands in uncouth Akō. Don't you know how to do anything correctly? You can't even kneel in the proper fashion. Put your knees exactly a fist-width apart. Your legs are so fat you probably can't even do that."

Asano struggled to his feet and screamed, "I've had enough of this. You're nothing but a self-important bakufu upstart."

Purple with rage he unsheathed his dagger and waved it in Kira's face. To avoid the sharp point wobbling menacingly near his nose Kira turned away. Asano brought the knife down clumsily and grazed the back of his head. Kira put his hand on the painful gash, inspected his bloody palm and beat a hasty retreat. Fuelled with rage Asano pursued his teacher with uncharacteristic energy. He struck again but missed his target and planted the dagger in a wooden column. While struggling to extract his weapon, he was grabbed by a court guard who had heard the ruckus in the classroom and rushed in to intervene in the squabble. The guard easily flipped Asano onto the floor and held him down by pressing his foot on the daimyo's neck.

Summoned by a shout more guards appeared and Asano was ordered to sit in the center of a circle of warriors. Kira relieved to see his attacker subdued ran off to the bakufu inspectors and reported what had happened. The Shogun's officials discussed the event and decided that because it was illegal to unsheathe a weapon in the castle there was sufficient reason to convene a meeting of bakufu justices the next day. In the meantime, they ordered that Asano was to be escorted from the castle and taken to a daimyo's house, and there to be held in custody. This was a common way of incarcerating individuals under criminal charges. As it would be dishonorable for a man of the samurai class to attempt escape. The holding of individuals, in what we would now call remand, was not an onerous task.

It wasn't long before the story of the attack became the topic of discussion on the streets of Edo. Almost immediately the events at the castle were adapted to a catchy song that mocked Asano's botched attempt to maintain his honor with clumsy, inept swordsmanship. The song entertained both the high and low classes in the city that at the time had a population of around one million.

The day after the attack the judicial authorities of the bakufu met to consider the evidence fully. In their verdict, they found Asano guilty of assault and condemned him to death by seppuku. This would have come as no surprise to him. Historians have concluded that Asano was well aware of the consequences of his impulsive and rash attack. They have unearthed documents that show that one of his family members had done the same thing in similar circumstanced and paid with performing seppuku. Anger management was not among the traits of members of this clan. In addition to the death sentence, Asano's estates were to be confiscated and distributed to other daimyo, and his corps of samurai warriors was to be disbanded. The Shoguns court concluded that the event involved unilateral misconduct, and they exonerated Kira. While his life was spared Kira lost face as a coward. His appointment at court was terminated, and his source of income was cut off.

Chapter 2: The Revenge Plot

After the ceremonial burial of Asano at Sengakuji temple, his samurai retrieved their horses and rode off to Akō. There they assembled to consider what they should do next. The chief samurai, 47-year-old Oishi Koranosuke, took charge and advised his fellow warriors to pursue a proper course of honor by killing Kira. The warriors were not bound to him as they had been relieved of their oath of loyalty with the death of Asano. They did, however, owe loyalty to the bushidō warrior code that obligated them to show courage, live a righteous life and maintain their honor. The death of their master insulted their honor and to save face they agreed that revenge was necessary.

The samurai discussed strategy for their vendetta and concluded that they would bide their time. It was rumoured that Kira had retreated to his home in Edo and surrounded himself with guards supplied by his wealthy father-in-law. The Akō warriors who were now rōnin wisely chose to disperse and re-group at some time in the future when it was clear that they could succeed in killing Kira.

In some of the many versions of the story, Oishi blamed himself for the tragedy. He regretted that he had not accompanied Asano to Edo but rather stayed in Akō to manage the daimyo's estates. If he had been with the master, he believed, the tragedy would not have occurred. Had he been in charge he would have ensured that proper gifts were offered to Kira who then would not have ceased provoking Asano. By plotting revenge Oishi was compensating for his personal failure and loss of honor.

The Akō rōnin parted company when Asano's estates were turned over to a new daimyo. Some of them went into the service of the new lord and the others moved to Edo and took up jobs as craftsmen and merchants. Oishi, their leader and master of the plot against Kira, moved to Kyoto with his wife and two sons. It is not clear what he did in terms of earning a living, but his behavior there was the subject of considerable interest to tellers of the various versions of the story of the 47 righteous rōnin.

In Kyoto Oishi sank into a dissolute life, drinking heavily and associating with prostitutes and rogues. It is implied in the legend that this behavior was feigned to lull Kira into believing he was safe, but there is historical evidence that Oishi was naturally inclined to inordinate imbibing in drink. In the matter of availing himself of the pleasures of sex in brothels, he was merely following the tastes of the day among all ranks of men. His error as reported by the more upright of the era and in the following periods may have been his habit of frequenting brothels offering hashijorō or prostitutes of the third rank. Kira justifiably apprehensive of retribution sent spies to Kyoto and they reported back to him details of Oishi's life including consorting with prostitutes unsuitable to his class.

In one episode of the legend, it is said that a man came upon Oishi lying in the street in a drunken stupor. He recognized the former head samurai of Asano's court and brutally addressed the snoring, debauched and smelly warrior.

"Faithless beast! Fool and craven!" he muttered, "you who are unworthy of the name of a samurai." He kicked Oishi face and ribs and tried to awaken him by bending to his ear and shouting, "aren't you the Oishi who once was a councillor of Asano Naganori? You haven't the heart to avenge your lord. You're a disgusting wastrel giving yourself up to women and wine."

As would be expected, Oishi's moral collapse had repercussions at home. His wife of 20 years became fed up and confronted him.

"My lord," she screamed at him, "you told me at first that your debauchery was a trick to make your enemy relax. But you have gone on with this far too long. I can't stand it anymore."

Oishi struck his wife in the face. While wiping her white lead makeup and blood from his hand, he angrily said that he was tired of her whining and complaining.

"If," he announced, "his life was not to her liking she should pack her bags and leave." "And what's more," he said "he was tired of looking at her old face." Seething with anger he bellowed, "I would be quite happy to marry a tayū (first class prostitute) and enjoy a life of unending pleasure."

Oishi's wife retreated to the next room, waited until he cooled down then apologized. But this proved fruitless as he demanded that she leave immediately and take the two boys and their infant daughter with her. The domestic squabble did not abate, and Oishi's wife soon left with their youngest son and daughter. Their eldest son Shikara, a teenager, chose to stay with his father.

The violent domestic row was dutifully reported to Kira whose spies were told the details of the rancorous separation by a neighbor. In the legend that grew around the plot of revenge Oishi was depicted as an honorable man who had sacrificed his wife and two children all in order to pursue vengeance on Kira and, if one is not generous, to have some fun while putting in the time. In doing this, he was forced to appear, as some said, to contravene the bushidō admonition of Imagawa Ryōshun who wrote "it is forbidden to be given up to drinking and carousing and a gambling life, in order to forget one's family duties." Oishi believed that the end justified the means so contravening his moral code was justified by his most honorable goal of revenge.

The vengeance driven rōnin residing in Edo having taken up a variety of trades managed to have one of their number, a carpenter, obtain the floor plan of Kira's mansion. He did this by courting and marrying the daughter of one of the craftsmen who had worked on the mansion. From information supplied by his father-in-law, the scheming rōnin was able to draw sketches of Kira's home. He added to the plan notes indicating where the guards were stationed within the walled compound and how many were at each post.

When the plotters in Edo were convinced that the time was ripe for attack they summoned Oishi. With his son, he surreptitiously departed from Kyoto eluding Kira's spies and joined his companion warriors in making final preparations for the assault. The rōnin had left their weapons and armor in the armory at Akō when they began their new life, so they set about rearming themselves surreptitiously so as to avoid the attention of rumor-mongers. Instead of buying new armor from a professional craftsman they made their own.

Oishi and his fellow plotters knew that the moment they put their plan into effect they were signing their own death warrants. For this, they were prepared by the bushidō code under which they had disciplined themselves to mediate daily on death. Their moral rules stated they must think carefully and often of death and the details of the many ways it could come to them; being ripped apart, drowned, burnt, struck by lightning, shaken to death by earthquake, falling from cliffs, dying of disease or committing seppuku at the death of their master. They were bound to ponder regularly what it would be like to be dead that is, dwelling in the concealed world. Only to the courageous was death unimportant.

Chapter 3: The Attack

When the rōnin decided on the exact day on which to launch their attack some of the band backed out of the proposed action. They lacked the courage to proceed as it was clear to everyone that no matter what happened all the active plotters were going to their deaths. A document that still exists today, was drawn up by the rōnin outlining the details of their intentions. The manifesto was necessary because they wanted others to know, should they fail in their task that their plot and actions were justified and honorable according to the bushidō code. A list was made of the 47 participants in the raid all of whom knew that if they failed to kill Kiri they would be executed as common criminals and if they succeeded in their quest expected to be condemned to seppuku as a reward for their loyalty to their master.

Before setting out the samurai squad cemented their commitment in a modest feast at a teahouse and all pledged to be unwavering in their actions and accept the fact that they would die the next day. They decided that if the bakufu officers interrupted the night's work they would refuse to come out of Kira's mansion until he was dead and if when they were leaving the house the neighbors interfered they would reveal what they had done and retreat to the temple of Ekōin and there await the arrival of the authorities. Oishi warned the group to avoid killing old men, women and children as it was dishonorable to kill the helpless.

With bellies full of rice and spirits high, the 47 men put on their inexpertly made armor and thrust their long and short swords specially fabricated for the attack into their sashes. The long swords were forged with blades a little longer than regulations allowed and their short swords were made with blades slightly smaller than normal to give them advantage in close quarters combat inside Kira's house. Some of the samurai put on quivers of arrows and carried a bow and others carried long spears. Four of them shouldered ladders and others held unlit torches. They were a rag-tag group in their homemade armor and odd assortment of weapons. The oldest of the group was Horibei Yahyoe Akizne age 77, and the youngest was Oishi son, Shikara aged 15. All were full-fledged samurai with the exception of Terasaka Kichiemon a low-ranking foot soldier or *ashigaru* bound by loyalty to his own master the rōnin Yoshida Chūzaemon.

At midnight December 13, 1702 the band set out on foot. It was a windy, snowy, cold night. They pushed quietly on from the teahouse through the blizzard to the Edo neighborhood where the mansions of the bakufu officials were located.

Reaching Kira's house the raiding party, following a prearranged plan, was divided into two. Oishi's son under the protection of the second highest ranking samurai, 64-year-old Yoshida Chūzaemon, and 22 others made their way to the rear gate. The rest assembled at the front. Ladders were silently placed against the compound walls and four men scampered up and using ropes let themselves down on the other side. They surprised the gatekeeper and his guards, tied them up and demanded the keys to the large double wooden doors of the main gate. The trussed up men all confirmed that they didn't have the keys that were kept inside the house. The raiders were forced to smash the iron lock on the gates and in doing so ended their stealth. Oishi fearing that the neighbors would be awakened by the noise and raise an alarm sent a messenger around to their houses explaining that the rōnin were not burglars but warriors avenging the death of their master. They assured the residents of the adjacent houses that they intended no harm to them. Kira's role as villain in the story as it spread through the city the following day was reinforced by the report that his neighbors detested him because he was miserly and self-important. Whether this was true or not, all of Kira's neighbors assured the messenger that they would do nothing to help him. Perhaps they were also swayed by the fact that the rōnin were attempting an honor killing.

Oishi gave the signal for 10 archers to climb the ladders to the top of the wall and make their way up to the tiled curved roofs surrounding the courtyard. According to the prearranged tactics they were stationed there so that they could shoot down any of Kira's guard who tried to run off and get help from his relatives.

When all his men were in position Oishi pounded on a drum giving the signal for the attack to begin. The samurai at the back of the house smashed in the door, and those at the front poured in through the gate, ran to the veranda and entered the house. The noise roused Kira. Sensing danger he ushered his wife and the female servants into a secluded room.

In the large reception room, the samurai were attacked by 10 guardsmen. Disregarding their own lives the combatants faced off and enaged in kenjutsu swordfights. Their agility and stamina had been perfected in years of practicing the craft of war through exercises or kata using bamboo swords or shinai. The paired engagements ended with the defeat of Kira's men whose hacked and bleeding bodies littered the floor. The rear party joined the main group and all the raiders engaged in close-quarter fights with the guards. They were handily dispatched under the watchful eye of Oishi who supervised the fray while sitting on a camp stool. Some of the guards escaped into the front courtyard and tried to run off and get help, but they were killed in a fusillade of arrows loosed from all sides by the archers on the roof.

To the dead, dying and wounded Oishi announced, "we have come only for our enemy Kira and we do not want you to shed any more blood for your master." However when the raiders approached Kira's private rooms three more guards furiously attacked and fought so skillfully that they pushed back the entire band of rōnin. Oishi spurred his warriors on saying, "did not every man of you swear to lay down his life in avenging his lord? How could you be held off by these three men?" "To die fighting," he told them, "in a master's cause should be the noblest ambition of a retainer." He located his son Shakira in the melee and ordered him to rush at the three defenders saying that if they were too strong he, as a true samurai, was to accept his own death.

Shikara lunged at the guards with a spear but was forced out into the courtyard by the fiercely fighting samurai Waku Handaiyu. Stepping back Shikara tripped and fell ignominiously into a fountain. Waku pursued him and raising his sword prepared to decapitate the soaking boy. Apparently helpless the young samurai with considerable skill twisted his body while swing his long sword and cut off his enemy's foot. The agile lad jumped from the fountain, swung his sword at Waku and severed his head. The rōnin inspired by Shikara's demonstration of courage redoubled their attack on the remaining guards and subdued them.

With Kira's men now dead or wounded, the raiders separated to search the house for the one they had come to kill. During the mop-up operation, Shikara discovered Kira's son hiding in a small chamber. Startled he was only able to wound him as he headed out the back door and fled into the night. The others found only women and children. There was no trace of Kira.

The disheartened samurai assembled in the main reception room and discussed the failure of their raid. They considered the option of ending their lives immediately. Oishi would have none of this defeatist talk. He ordered his men to make one more sweep of the house, and he himself went into Kira's sleeping chamber. He bent down and felt the quilt on the sleeping mat and shouted out to his men "as the quilt is warm the enemy must be nearby."

Encouraged by this news the rōnin crowded into the room and examined it carefully. Behind a scroll hung on the wall a hole was discovered. They poked spears into the darkness behind and found no resistance. Holding a torch Yazma Jiutaro entered the hole and discovered a passage leading to a courtyard. It was empty, but on one side he saw a little woodshed. On inspecting, the building by the light of his torch saw something white. He poked it with his spear. Two men jumped out and attacked him. They were soon put out of action by a band of warriors that had followed Yazma through the secret passage. He went back to the woodshed and jabbed his spear about again. From under a pile of quilts he heard a squeal. Pushing the bedding aside he discovered a man lying on his back and bleeding from a wound in the thigh. He reached down to pull the man out of the shed but found himself facing threatened by a slashing dagger. A blow to the wrist sent the weapon flying, and Yazma dragged the man by the feet into the courtyard and placed his foot on his neck.

The ronin gathered around the prisoner who stayed mute even when they poked him with their spears. He looked to them to be of the noble class and of about 60 years of age. He was dressed a white silk sleeping robe fashioned from expensive fabric. They demanded his name over and over, but he remained silent. Suspecting that they had achieved their goal they gave the whistle signal that had been agreed upon beforehand would indicate the capture of Kira.

Oishi and the rest of the samurai made their way to the courtyard. With a lantern in hand, he inspected the captured man and seeing the scar from a cut on his neck confirmed his identity.

Oishi knelt down and examined the trembling prisoner. "My lord exalted person" he said, honoring his enemy's high rank, "we are the samurai of Asano Naganori. Many months ago you quarrelled with our master, and he was sentenced to seppuku and his family was ruined."

"He was found guilty of attacking me by the bakufu justices," Kira spluttered.

"Nevertheless," replied Oishi, "we have come to avenge him. You must acknowledge the justice of our cause."

"I will no such thing. You broke the law by entering my house," Kira said indignantly. "There is not one speck of justice in your cause."

Oishi exhaled audibly. He asked Kira politely to perform seppuku. He even offered to serve as his second and promised to administer the coup de grace with efficiency and honor. Kiri shook his head.

The courtesy of an honorable death appropriate to a nobleman was proposed to him a second, third and fourth time. He steadfastly refused these offers.

Exercising the greatest courtesy two rōnin knelt down and firmly held Kira's arms and legs while Oishi drew from beneath his kimono the seppuku knife with which Asano had ended his life. He knelt beside Kira and with the razor-sharp blade sliced off his head. Gingerly avoiding the gush of blood Oishi grasped the knot of hair at the back of Kira's head and held it aloft so that all the rōnin could see the fruit of their laborious planning and exhausting battle. The head was passed to the nearest warrior. He raised it again for all to see then dropped it in the wooden bucket brought along by the raiders for the purpose of carrying the object they had waited so long to obtain.

Before departing the house Oishi ordered that the samurai go around and extinguish all the torches and open fires. This was necessary to protect the neighborhood of highly flammable wood houses from the kind of conflagration that regularly engulfed residential Edo. Leaving unattended fires, torches and lanterns was considered an offence in Japan.

At dawn, December 14th, Oishi's samurai left Kira's house. They had placed a copy of their manifesto in a box on a pole so that anyone entering the scene of battle would not miss it. They walked to the nearby Ekōin temple where they had planned to commit mass suicide, however, the priest at the gate would not let them in. It was too early he said. For the rōnin, voluntary seppuku was the most honorable death as it was performed without the aid of a swordsman to render death relatively painless by swift decapitation. The obstinate temple gate-keeper was not swayed in his determination to keep them out no matter how much they argued with him.

With their plans necessarily changed, the band set off for the Sengakuji temple. Oishi carrying the bucket containing their trophy led the solomn procession through the residential district of Edo. The samurai were apprehensive expecting an attack from the rear by warriors loyal to Kira's wealthy father-in-law. One of the 18 daimyo of Japan serving his period of residency in Edo saw the procession on the street in front of his mansion. He had been one of those in charge of the training of the young Asano, and when he heard what had transpired was so pleased with 47 rōnin that he ordered his samurai to march out and join the procession and protect them. Along the way another daimyo Matsudaira Mutsu the Prince of Sendai took pity on the bedraggled and exhausted rōnin and invited them into his home for a meal. They were served gruel and wine and praised by everyone in the household. Thus fortified, Oishi's samurai proceeded on their journey.

Chapter 4: The Aftermath

On arriving at the Buddist temple of Sengakuji, the rōnin were met by the priests who escorted them to a well where the head of Kira was washed. They took it to the grave of Asano and offered it to their former master who was, according to their beliefs, present as a dweller in the concealed world of the dead. They also placed on the grave a copy of their statement of purpose with a roll call list of all those who had participated in the act of retribution. Oishi, then Shikara and all the other rōnin in turn read a prayer and burned incense at Asano's tomb. The plan for the raid and its aftermath being meticulous Oishi had under his kimono a sack of money. He handed this to the chief priest and asked him to ensure that after the 47 had performed seppuku their bodies would be buried with dignity and that prayers be said over their graves.

Two of Oishi's men were sent to the Shogun's chief inspector with a third copy of the manifesto to announce that the death of Asano had now been avenged. The rest of the warriors seated themselves on the ground and discussed their fate. Some favored immediate seppuku and others wanted to humble themselves before the Shogun's justices and have the honor of accepting their decision as to the means of death either seppuku by decree or execution as common criminals. By surrendering to the Shogun, the rōnin were to demonstrate their allegiance to their ultimate master.

A contingent of the Shogun's guard arrived at the temple and placed the group of plotters, sitting passively on the ground, under arrest. In the castle, a council of bakufu justices met and ordered that the plotters be divided into four groups and placed in the custody of four daimyo. The senor 17 rōnin were sent to the house of Hosokawa from the domain of Kuamoto and groups of 10 were allocated to the mansions of lesser daimyo. At the Hosokawa mansion one of the principal retainers, a certain Horiuchi Den'emon, engaged the interned rōnin in discussion as they were awaiting judgement. He wrote down the substance of their conversations held over several days. Acting as a kind of journalist he asked for and was given a copy of the plotters statement of purpose and was given a list of the men involved in the attack. His account of what had happened would be of considerable importance in later historical research on the event.

The justices of the bakufu considered the question of the proper way to dispose of Kira's assassins. On the one hand, the rōnin had followed the way of bushidō by avenging the death of their master, and for this they deserved to be honored but, on the other hand, they had committed a criminal offence by contravening the authority of the Shogun, engaging in a plot for revenge and disturbing the peace of Edo. Their deliberations were made even more difficult as petitions flowed in from admirers of the loyalty of the rōnin to their deceased master. It was decided that rather than die dishonorably decapitated as common criminals, the plotters would be honored by condemnation to perform seppuku. In order to spread some of the blame for the affair, the justices roundly criticized Kira's relatives for their failure to provide adequate protection to the former retainer in the Shogun's court.

In the early morning of March 20, 1703, the courtyards of four daimyo mansions were prepared with mats laid down in a row. On the left of each mat was a small stand holding a seppuku knife and on the right a bowl with a piece of cloth. The condemned entered the courtyards followed by their seconds chosen by them from among the daimyo's skilled swordsmen. In each of the four houses, the same ritual was performed. As if in a choreographed dance, the rōnin knelt in unison, took up the knives and pieces of cloth, wrapped the fabric and their hands around the upper part of the blade and disembowelled themselves. The swords of the samurai seconds swung simultaneously, and the row of the condemned men's torsos fell forward.

The bodies were taken in procession from the four mansions through the streets lined by crowds of onlookers. The funeral parties converged at the Sengakuji temple. The bodies of the rōnin were ceremoniously transferred to the priests who washed the corpses, prayed, burned incense and prepared the loyal samurai for burial next to the tomb of their master Asano.

Stone markers were erected to commemorate the resting place of each of the rōnin. It wasn't long before crowds flocked to the cemetery to pray at the graves of Asano and his loyal retainers. Among their number was the man who has kicked and insulted the drunken Oishi passed out in a Kyoto gutter.

He prostrated himself on Oishi's grave and wailed, "forgive me most loyal samurai. Had I known that you were awaiting a propitious moment to revenge the death of your master I would not have treated you so badly. I failed to honor you then as I should have, but I honor you now." As soon as he had uttered these words of regret he pulled a dagger from under his kimono, sliced open his belly first from left to right and then vertically. With his eyes never losing their focus on the tombstone, disembowelled he fell dead a full minute later. The priests of Sengakuji buried him next to Oishi and the rōnin thus granting him the honor of a deserving bushidō warrior.

Chapter 5: The Legacy

The small temple of Sengakuji becomes a hive of activity each year on December 14 when a major festival is held to commemorate the 47 rōnin also known as Akō Gishi-sai. Crowds flow into the small graveyard where they burn quantities incense before the markers of the heroic warriors. If it is a windless day, the air becomes dense with the smoke. A parade with people dressed as rōnin wends its way to the temple and special festive food is served at stands in the streets. Gishi-sai is a celebration of the virtues of honor, loyalty and sacrifice epitomized by the story of the courageous 47 masterless samurai.

Most of the year the temple is quiet with visitors solemnly making their way up to the well where Kira's head was washed and then moving on into the graveyard. A small memorial museum, opened in 2001, sits in the temple precinct. There visitors can inspect the homemade armor worn by the rōnin and the drum beaten by Oishi on the night of the raid on Kira's house. Among the documents on display is the signed receipt for Kira's head handed over to his family after resting on Asano's tomb.

How the story of the 47 rōnin evolved from an historical event into a legend known by all in Japan provides an intriguing insight into the changing ideas of the bushidō code of virtuous behavior. In 1990s Akō the hometown of the rōnin became embroiled in a public debate over the historical truth of the actual number of samurai who committed seppuku three centuries before.

Terasaka Kichiemon, the lowest ranking of the samurai, was to be among those held under custody in the mansion of the daimyo Mizuno, but he seems to have disappeared. When questioned his immediate master Yoshida Chūzaemon, second-in-command of the raid, said that Terasaka left the group at the gate to Kira's house and hence did not participate in the attack. "In any case," he said, "Terasaka was of no concern." He was not among the rōnin who performed seppuku. If this is true and careful examination of the historical evidence suggests that it is, the number of rōnin should be set at 46. The dispute in Akō over the actual number of rōnin involving scholars, local historians and priests reached city hall where council decided that for the purposes of official ceremonies and tourist events, the number would be kept at 47.

The problem with Terasaka and what role he played in the plot became confused from the 18th century on because the story of the 47 rōnin developed into a popular subject in various forms of public entertainment. Two contradictory stories persisted in the burgeoning legend of the rōnin. In one, he is pictured as a coward who ran away just before the attack. In the other, he served in a secret mission. Ordered Oishi in this version Terasaka escaped detention and hurried to Hiroshima with a report on the success of the enterprise to be delivered to Asano Daigaku the brother of Asano Naganori. In an imaginative chronicle written in 1703, it was stated that Terasaka was elevated to the rank of full samurai or shibun when Kira's head was delivered to the tomb of Asano. After running off to Akō and Hiroshima as a messenger, he returned to Edo and asked the Shogun's chief inspector to be condemned to death by seppuku claiming that he was as guilty as his lately deceased fellow samurai. His request was denied. He served as a retainer to the descendants of his deceased master Yoshida Chūzaemon until his death in 1747.

The incredible afterlife or life after death of the 47 rōnin spanning three centuries must please them as honor flows down to them in the concealed world. A mere two weeks after their bodies were tucked away underground their heroic deed was adapted as the subject of a kabuki play. Although the characters names were replaced by pseudonyms, the bakufu authorities shut down the production. Three years later a puppet play also with the names changed was performed in Edo. To protect against censorship the characters were given the names of samurai from a much earlier era, but everyone in the audience would have been able to understand from the action that, for example, a puppet named Kō no Morano, a 14th century samurai, was actually meant to represent Kira.

After the death of Shogun Tsunayoshi in 1709, the gates opened for a flood of interest in the tale now openly titled *The Forty-Seven Loyal Retainers in Akō*, as it appeared on stage and in puppet theaters. Not only could the subject be presented without disguise but a public decree went out that granted pardon to the heirs of the rōnin and Asano, as well. The habit of hiding the names of the rōnin, however, persisted, and the stories of the individuals involved were expanded and modified to include a raft of completely imaginative adventures. There were so many stage productions telling different stories in the years around 1710 that historians of popular Japanese entertainment describe this period as an Akō boom.

Fictional versions of the tale of the rōnin known as chūshingura increased in popularity throughout the 18th century. The most influential of them was a puppet play Kanadehon Chūshingura first performed in 1748 in Osaka. The title means "Kana practice book treasure of the loyal retainers." Kana are the 47 Japanese syllabic characters, so the play combined the system of writing with the number rōnin. There was no dispute over their number at this time. That was to come later with the rise of detail-oriented nitpickers practicing "scientific" historical research.

In the Kanadehon Chūshingura Terasaka appears in Act VII as a character named Heiemon, a simple disguised form of his real name Kichiemon. In the midst of the action which involves a melodramatic plot he says "The sad thing about being of the lower ranks is that unless you prove to the other samurai your spirit is better than theirs, they won't let you join them." Of course in the play, he proves himself and is allowed to join the other rōnin as a full-fledged member of their cabal. The message here is that even those of the lower ranks can, with perseverance and commitment to the bushidō way of life, raise themselves up the social ladder. Terasaka's new status allows him the right to perform seppuku with the others. This is a fine inspiring story that people still love today even if they know that Terasaka is recorded as living as a retainer after 1703 that he survived to the age of eighty-three and even if they have seen his tomb next to that of his wife at the Sōkeiji Temple in Azabu.

With the rise of historical scholarship in Japan based on the 19th century German model of systematic research and the publication of the primary documents on the Akō rōnin, the various meanings of the story and its moral content began to be debated. The judgement of the Shogun's justices was examined carefully. Should the rōnins' undisputed loyalty and adherence to the morals demanded in bushidō or samurai life have trumped the criminal law of the era that forbade vendettas? Did the Shogun's court follow bushidō precepts in exonerating Kira for his failure to demonstrate courage? The conclusions of the historians were as much based on the virtues demanded of Japanese society at the time of their writing than on impartial consideration of justice in the early 18th century. Terasaka was condemned as a coward by some and praised for his loyalty by those who chose to believe that he had asked the bakufu officials to condemn him to seppuku.

At the same time as modern historical scholarship was developing in Japan the story of the rōnin was taken up by a growing number of storytellers who entertained their audiences with tales of revenge. The Gishi tales were also extremely popular with street performers until they were forced from their stalls in a late 19th century move for urban renewal in Tokyo. The tales of the Gishi did not appear in print for a wide readership until the 1850s.

The many stories embellishing the slender historical facts of the lives and adventures of the 47 rōnin were adapted by a new kind of public entertainment in the late 19th century that arose in the slums of Tokyo. The Naniwabushi were singing poets whose narratives delighted at first the common folk on the street and then later were immensely popular in legitimate theaters. The most famous performer of this form of art was Tōchūken Kumoemon whose repertoire in the early 20th century was primarily narratives of the 47 righteous samurai of Akō or Akō Gishi. He called himself a promoter of bushidō which became an essential element in raising militarism among the Japanese during the Sino-Japanese war of 1894-5 and the Russo-Japanese War of 1904-5. It was through the re-birth of interest in samurai culture that the Japanese were led to believe that pursuit of military virtues was a quality of the Japanese race. The rōnins' story went hand in hand with the notion of a bushidō renaissance. This was promoted by surviving members of the samurai class who wanted to modernize the practice of martial arts and interestingly by missionaries who equated bushidō virtues with Christian virtues.

As Naniwabushi declined in popularity, the legend of the rōnin was given new life in film and then television. In the presentation of silent films, the legend of the Akō Gishi was recited or sung by a professional entertainer as the story appeared on the screen. Between the 1930s and 1960s a whole slew of Gishi films were made some of which attempted to achieve a historic validity through accurate period costuming and staging. The tradition continued in television productions that tell and retell versions of the heroic lives of the righteous rōnin from Akō. It is impossible to escape the legend as it becomes essential programming on Japanese television in December each year. The afterlife of the rōnin in film shows no signs of abating. Their story is in almost continuous production in Japanese cinema and television. One of the most readily available of these is the films is the *The Loyal 47 Ronin* directed by Kunio Watanabe released in 1958 and available with English subtitles. In the west, the story may just be getting started. Whether the long-awaited film *47 Ronin,* starring Keanu Reeves and several Japanese movie stars will inaugurate a rōnin boom in North America remains to be seen.

With the rise of modern historical research in Japan in the 19th century and the publication of the original documents on the Akō rōnin Japanese historical novelists jumped on the popular story. They invariably used the real names for the characters to suggest that their stories were more truthful than the traditional Chūshingura or stories of the loyal retainers. The many novels written about the rōnin are of varying quality some readable and many more entirely forgettable. One can expect a similar enthusiasm for the subject in the English speaking world if the Keanu Reeves film has the impact that its promoters have promised. Even without the inspiration of a film the rōnin have had a good afterlife in English fiction. A popular fantasy comic book series written and drawn by Frank Miller was published between 1983 and 1984 and they have been republished several times. A novel *The Ronin* by William Jennings published 2007 set the story is set in the 12th century thus carrying on the tradition in Japan of moving the tale backward in time. More recently the story has been retold a Shogunate detective novel *The Rōnin's Mistress* (2011) by Laura Joh Rowland in (2011).

Why are the righteous rōnin, also known in the west as the masterless samurai of Akō and the loyal retainers, so enduring in popularity? For the Japanese their story has been used as an example of unquestioning loyalty, virtue struggling against corruption of the state and ideal military and civilian behavior especially perseverance and honor. The same virtues and righteousness appealed to audiences in the English speaking world right from the first presentation of the story in the once popular *Tales of Old Japan* by A.B. Mitford in published in 1871. The story of the 47 rōnin has had the power to move generations of readers and filmgoers in much the same way as the legend of Robin Hood.

For the modern westerner, there is something quaint about the adherence to fixed principles of morality. This is not true for all as these are an integral part of the training of athletes in the martial art of kendo, a modern version of the kenjutsu style used by the 47 rōnin in dispatching Kira's samurai. One would be hard-pressed today to find an employee who would sacrifice his job to seek retribution for the firing of his boss. There is something beyond moral instruction that keeps the tale of the rōnin appealing to the public. The market for comics, novels, films and video games such as *Usagi Yojimbo, The Way of the Ronin* suggests that the violence in kenjutsu martial arts as practiced by the samurai originally using razor-sharp swords and resulting with lots of blood-spilling is universally entertaining especially to the young male.

In the west, there has always been a fascination with the motif of seppuku in Japanese history and literature. The idea that the blemishes of corruption and failure can be eradicated, and personal honor restored through voluntary seppuku is inherently intriguing. Further, the western reader or filmgoer cannot avoid contemplating the actual seppuku ritual. The painful process of seppuku, particularly without a swordsman second, requiring unbelievable fortitude is for westerners a fascinating exotic practice. The discipline of one performing seppuku particularly in maintaining the composure necessary to make a second vertical cut to the belly is truly astounding. For a westerner, it is an astounding way restore one's honor. It is of a totally different order than the unceremonious bullet-to-the-head method of suicide practiced by the likes of Hitler and Hemingway.

Bibliography

Daidōji, Yūsan. **Code of the Samurai: A Modern Translation of the Bushidō Shoshinshū.** North Clarendon VT, Tuttle Pub. 1999.

Freeman-Mitford, Algernon Bertram. **Tales of Old Japan.** London: 1871 available at **Internet Archive**

Naganori, Asano. in **The Samurai Archives**

Hall, John Whitney, editor. **The Cambridge History of Japan.** Vol. 4 Early Modern Japan. Cambridge University Press, 1991.

Preston, Ted M. "The Stoic Samurai," **Asian Philosophy.** 13, 2003. Pp. 39-52, 2003

Ryōshun, Imagawa. The Regulations of Imagawa Ryōshun in **Wikisource**

Smith II, Harry D. "The Trouble with Terasaka: The Forty-Seventh Rōnin and the Chūshingura Imagination." **Japan Review** 16, 2004**. Pp.**3-65. **pdf**

Smith II, Harry D. "Singing Tales of the Gishi: Naniwabushi and the Forty-seven Rōnin in Late Meiji Japan." **Monumenta Nipponica.** Winter 2006. Pp. 459-508. **pdf**

Smith II, Harry D. "The Media and Politics of Japanese Popular History: The Case of the Akō Gishi." In Baxter, James C. ed. **Historical Consciousness, Historiography, and Modern Japanese Values.** Kyoto: International Research Center for Japanese Studies, 2006. Pp. 75-97. **pdf**

Weinberg, David R. Kuniyoshi. **The Faithful Samurai.** Leiden, 2005.

Made in the USA
Las Vegas, NV
01 December 2022

60836629R00036